This bo~~ok belongs to~~

I celebrated World Book Day 20
with this brilliant gift
from my local Bookseller,
Hachette Children's Group,
Francesa Simon and Tony Ross.

First published in Great Britain in 2016
by Hodder and Stoughton

1 3 5 7 9 10 8 6 4 2

Text © Francesca Simon, 2005, 2006, 2007, 2008, 2009, 2010, 2014, 2015
Illustrations © Tony Ross, 2005, 2006, 2007, 2008, 2009, 2010, 2014, 2015

The moral rights of the author and illustrator have been asserted.

A CIP catalogue record for this book
is available from the British Library.

ISBN 978 1 5101 0279 8
ISBN 978 1 5101 0349 8 (Export)

Printed and bound by CPI Group (UK) Ltd, Croydon, CR0 4YY

The paper and board used in this book are from well-managed forests
and other responsible sources.

MIX
Paper from
responsible sources
FSC® C104740

The Hachette Children's Group would like to thank Stora Enso Anjala Mill,
Finland and Paper Management Services for their contribution
to the paper used for this World Book Day printing.

Orion Children's Books
An imprint of
Hachette Children's Group
Part of Hodder and Stoughton
Carmelite House
50 Victoria Embankment
London EC4Y 0DZ

An Hachette UK Company

www.hachette.co.uk
www.hachettechildrens.co.uk
www.horridhenry.co.uk

Francesca Simon
Illustrated by Tony Ross

HORRiD HENRY

FUNNY Fact Files

Orion
Children's Books

This book has been specially written and published to celebrate 20 years of World Book Day. For further information, visit www.worldbookday.com.
World Book Day in the UK and Ireland is made possible by generous sponsorship from National Book Tokens, participating publishers, authors, illustrators and booksellers. Booksellers who accept the £1* World Book Day Book Token bear the full cost of redeeming it.

World Book Day, World Book Night and Quick Reads are annual initiatives designed to encourage everyone in the UK and Ireland — whatever your age — to read more and discover the joy of books and reading for pleasure. World Book Night is a celebration of books and reading for adults and teens on 23 April, which sees book gifting and celebrations in thousands of communities around the country: www.worldbooknight.org
Quick Reads provides brilliant short new books by bestselling authors to engage adults in reading: www.quickreads.org.uk

* €1.50 in Ireland

Greetings, Purple Hand Gang members and Henry fans!
You've all read loads of my adventures, but don't you ever
wonder what happened AFTER the stories ended?
Well, now you can find out.

I've written loads and loads of extra-special, top-secret,
brilliant, spectacular, fantastic facts. After you've read this
book, you'll know more about me than I do. See pages from my
diary! Discover my worst school dinner. How I get rid of evil
enemies. My best poem (hint — it's called I'M GONNA THROW
UP). How to tell if anyone you know is a zombie vampire. My
nature guide so you never step off concrete. I've even
included that worm-face, bossy-boots Margaret's sleepover
rules — just so you know NEVER to let her darken your
doorstep. And my story writing tips. And my autobiography.

See, I told you this book has everything. Soon I'll be your
Mastermind subject.

MWAHHHHHAAAAAHHHAAAAAAA

Happy reading from

Henry

THE TRUE AUTOBIOGRAPHY OF HENRY

Lord High Excellent Majesty of the Purple Hand Gang, leader and boss of the secret fort and the destroyer of the Secret Club and Nappy Noodle Brothers. Wizard, star actor, footballer, trickster, genius, the scourge of evil enemies and the bulldozer of babysitters and battle-axes and demon dinner ladies and horrible cousins.

I was born in February – oh let's skip that boring bit – to the King and Queen, but sadly I was stolen by an evil wizard and dumped with… THEM. Obviously I am waiting for my real parents to collect me and take me back to the palace, but until then I am stuck with the world's most boring, mean and horrible parents in the history of the world.

To say
nothing of their
son, the worm, my
so-called younger brother,
Peter. As if someone as
amazing as me could have such a nappy
noodle poopy pants for a brother. That just
proves I must have been stolen by a wizard.
There is no other possible explanation.

My greatest talent, among so many, is that I
am a genius trickster. I have played so many
amazing, fantastic tricks that it's hard even
for me to remember them all. I'll tell you
about some of them later on ...

by
Henry

HORRiD HENRY'S Year

HAPPY BiRTHDAY HENRY

February is my favourite
month — it's my
birthday, which means
loads of PRESENTS!

I got Mum the
perfect gift for
Mother's day.

Burying wormy worm Peter in the sand!

I love Halloween — an entire day devoted to stuffing your face with sweets and playing horrid tricks.

Christmas is all about getting more than you give!

King Henry the Horrible's Fact File

* *

Worst subjects:
Miss Battle-Axe
Moody Margaret
Stuck-up Steve
Perfect Peter
Mrs Oddbod

Best banquet:
TO START
Chocolate yum-yums

MAIN COURSES
Pizza
Burgers
Chips
Chocolate

DESSERTS
Chocolate ice cream
Chocolate cake
Chocolate biscuits
Fudge

Worst banquet:
TO START
Spinach tart

MAIN COURSES
Brussels sprouts
Cauliflower
Mussels
Tripe

DESSERTS
Fresh fruit
Chef had his head
chopped off

Best punishments:

Piranha-infested moat

Snakepit

Man-eating crocodiles

Scorpion cage

Best law:

Parents have to go to school, not children

Worst crimes:

Saying the word 'chores'

Setting homework

Bedtime

Best throne:

Comfy black chair

Worst throne:

School chair

Best regal robes:

Terminator Gladiator dressing-gown

Worst regal robes:

Pageboy outfit

Best palace:

300 rooms with 300 TVs

HORRID HENRY'S School Fact File

* *

Best friend:
Rude Ralph

Worst enemy:
Moody Margaret

Worst school dinner:
Lumpy surprise with lumps

Best school dinner:
Chips with chips

Worst subject:
Spelling
Maths
P.E.
History
Etc.

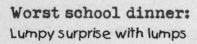

Favourite subject:
Lunch

Best book:
The Mummy's Curse

Worst book:
The Happy Nappy

Best poem:
'I'm Gonna Throw Up'

Most boring school trip:
Our town museum

Prizes:
Trophy for winning the cross-country run
on Sports Day
Family ticket to Book World for winning the
reading competition

Badge:
5 metre swimming badge

Best day in school:
Getting rid of Mr Nerdon

Worst days in school:
Being moved to the top spelling group
Wearing girls' pants

Happiest moment:
Sending Miss Battle-Axe to the Head

Scariest moments:
Injections

Nitty Nora's inspection

Worst time in the week:
Monday, 8.00 am

Best time in the week:
Friday, 3.30 pm

HORRID HENRY'S
Top Secret Fact file

* *

Best parties:
Pirate Parties

Cannibal curse parties

Terminator Gladiator
parties

Best Wedding:
NONE!

Best Dinner Guests:
Terminator Gladiator

Mutant Max

Marvin the Maniac

Tapioca Tina

Rapper Zapper

Battle-Axe

Worst parties:
Sammy the Snail party

Daffy and her Dancing
Daisies party

Princess party

Worst wedding:
Marrying Miss
Battle-Axe

Worst Dinner Guests:

Miss Battle-Axe

Stuck-Up Steve

Demon Dinner Lady

Best Revenge:

Telling Peter there were fairies at the bottom of the garden

Making Peter believe he was famous in the future

Getting Bossy Billy into trouble

Making Steve think there were monsters under the bed

Worst Revenge:

Peter sending Margaret a letter signed 'Henry' asking her to marry him (uggh)

Best Hike:

Walking between the comfy black chair and the fridge

Worst Hike:

Anywhere outdoors

Best sleepovers:
Eating all the ice cream at Greedy Graham's

Breaking all the beds at Dizzy Dave's

Staying up all night at Rude Ralph's

Worst sleepovers:
New Nick

Stuck-Up Steve

Moody Margaret nabbing my room

Worst will:
Mine

Best will:
Anyone leaving me lots of loot

Best restaurants:
Gobble and Go

Whopper Whoopee

Fat Frank's

Worst restaurants:
Restaurant Le Posh

Virtuous Veggie

HORRID HENRY'S Diary

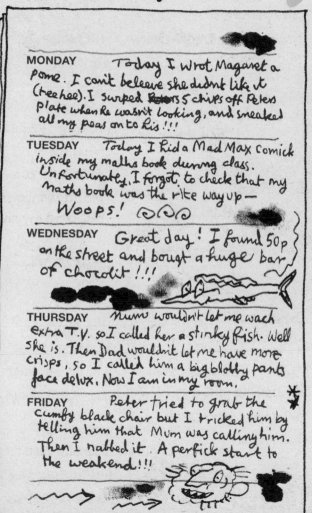

MONDAY   Today I wrot Magaret a pome. I cant beleeve she didnt like it (tee hee). I surped ~~Peters~~ 5 chips off Peters plate when he wasnt looking, and sneaked all my peas on to his !!!

TUESDAY   Today I hid a Mad Max comick inside my maths book during class. Unfortunatly, I forgot to check that my maths book was the rite way up — Woops! ∞∞∞

WEDNESDAY   Great day! I found 50p on the street and bougt a huge bar of chocolit !!!

THURSDAY   Mum wouldn't let me wach extra T.V. so I called her a stinky fish. Well she is. Then Dad wouldnt let me have more crisps, so I called him a big blobby pants face delux. Now I am in my room.

FRIDAY   Peter tried to grab the cumfy black chair but I tricked him by telling him that Mum was calling him. Then I nabbed it. A perfick start to the weakend!!!

HORRID HENRY'S Favourite Poem

* *

I'M GONNA THROW UP

Pirates puke on stormy seas
Giants spew on top of trees.
Kings are sick in golden loos
Dogs throw up on Daddy's shoes.

Babies love to make a mess
Down the front of Mum's best dress.
And what car ride would be complete
Without the stink of last night's treat?

Teachers who force kids to eat
Shepherd's pie with rancid meat
Can't be surprised when at their feet
The upchucked meal splats complete.

Rollercoasters, swirling cups
Can make anyone throw up.
Ferris wheels, icky sweets,
Pavement pizzas spray the streets.

Hats are handy when in town
Should your guts flip upside down.
A bag's a fine and private place
To avoid public disgrace
When, tummy heaving, insides peeling,
You suddenly get that awful feeling –
'Mum! I'm gonna throw up!'

If you're caught short while at sea
Don't worry! You'll die eventually.
But I for one do not believe
That bobbing ships cause folk to heave.
Sitting at the Captain's table
I scoffed as much as I was able.
I ate so many lovely dishes –
URGHHH! Now it's time to
feed the fishes.

HORRID HENRY'S
Home fact file

* *

Parents:
Mum and Dad

Brothers:
One horrible
younger brother,
Perfect Peter

Cousins:
Stuck-up Steve
Prissy Polly
Pimply Paul
Vomiting Vera

Grandparents:
Grandma
Grandpa

Catchphrase:
Out of my way, worm!

Hobbies:
Eating sweets
collecting gizmos

Aunts:
Rich Aunt Ruby
Great-Aunt Greta

Pets:
Fang (hamster)
Fluffy (cat)

Pocket money:
50p per week
(much too little)

Favorite sweets:
Big Boppers
Nose Pickers
Dirt Balls

Worst sweets:
None

Favourite food:
Crisps
Chocolate
Pizza

Worst Food:
Vegetables
Muesli

Favourite smell:
Pancakes

Favourite places:
Whopper Whoopee
Gobble and Go
Toy Heaven

Favourite TV programmes:
Gross-Out
Rapper Zapper
Mutant Max
Terminator Gladiator
Hog House

Worst TV programmes:
Manners with Maggie

Daffy and her
Dancing Daisies

Favourite pop groups:
Driller Cannibals

Killer Boy Rats

Favourite computer games:
Intergalactic Killer Robots

Snake Masters

Revenge III

Worst computer games:
Be a Spelling Champion

Virtual Classroom

Whoopee for Numbers

Best present:
Pancakes

Worst present:
Frilly pink lacy underpants

Worst Punishment:
No TV for a week

Greatest ambition:
To be crowned
King Henry the Horrible

Top Tips to Stop Annoying Little Brothers and Sisters Invading Your Room

Leave your oldest, stinkiest socks, dirty clothes and empty food wrappers everywhere – your room will be so messy that not even horrible little brothers and sisters will want to come in.

Pretend there's a terrifying Fangmangler living under your bed that likes to eat younger brothers and sisters. Be sure to make scary noises every time they pass your room.

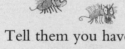

Tell them you have nits – they won't want to come anywhere near you and your creepy crawly friends!

Set up lots of booby traps – place a bucket of water over the door, make tricky tripwires out of string and set up your Goo-shooter to attack any sneaky invaders!

In case your invader manages to escape all your traps and reaches your top secret treasure drawer, place the following note inside.

KEEP OUT

You should be ashamed of yourself.

I am so disappointed that a relative of mine could be so sneaky.

Turn back before it's too late.

And never do it again!

My secret camera is filming you ...

HORRID HENRY'S
Family fact file

(All the stuff they don't want anyone to know!!!)

* *

SECRET DREAMS

Henry:
To be a dictator and rule the world

Peter:
To marry Miss Lovely

Mum:
To be a tap dancer

Dad:
To be a Rock'n'Roll god

Aunt Ruby:
To be best friends
with the Queen

Stuck-Up Steve:
To be a champion skier

Fluffy:
To live in a house filled with mice

Fang:
To be bigger than Fluffy

DEEPEST, DARKEST

Mum:
She sneaks sweets from a sweet jar

Dad:
He is scared of injections

Peter:
Miss Lovely once told him off
for running in class

Stuck-Up Steve:
He can't sleep without Little Ducky

Henry:
Wouldn't you like to know!

Perfect Peter's Top Secret Fairy Notes

What to do when you meet a fairy

1. Fairies are shy, so always whisper
2. Walk on tiptoe
3. Dress up as one yourself
4. Cover yourself in glitter
5. Choose a fairy name for yourself like Blossom

Remember, Fairy Liquid is not for fairies!

EVIL ENEMIES FACT FILE

* *

Peter

Nickname: Perfect

Worst features: too many to count

Best feature: none

Most evil crime: being born

Margaret

Nickname: Moody

Worst features: grouchy, bossy

Best feature: owns a pirate hook, sabre and cutlass

Most evil crime: living next door

Susan

Nickname: Sour

Worst feature: whining, moaning copycat

Best feature: slaps Margaret

Most evil crime: joining Margaret's secret club

Steve

Nickname: Stuck-up

Worst feature: always bragging about how rich he is

Best feature: lives far away

Most evil crime: trying to trick me into thinking his house was haunted

Bill

Nickname: Bossy

Worst feature: mean, double-crossing creep

Best feature: doesn't go to my school

Most evil crime: getting me into trouble at Dad's office

Rebecca

Nickname: Rabid

Worst features: toughest teen in town. Makes children go to bed early and hogs the TV.

Best feature: scared of spiders

Most evil crime: making me go to bed at 7 pm!!

Lily

Nickname: Lisping

Worst feature: follows me around

Best feature: smaller than me

Most evil crime: asking me to marry her

Worst babysitter

Tetchy Tess
Crabby Chris
Angry Anna
Rabid Rebecca

Other things I hate

Homework
Boring holidays
Walks
Fresh air
Healthy food
Bedtime

Greatest victories

Tricking Bossy Bill into photocopying
his bottom

Switching Christmas presents with
Stuck-up Steve

Stinkbombing Moody Margaret's
Secret Club

Enlisting Sour Susan as a double agent

Defeating Rabid Rebecca

Escaping Lisping Lily

Being older, bigger and cleverer than
Perfect Peter

HOW TO GET RID OF EVIL ENEMIES

Catapult them into a moat filled
with piranha fish

Let crocodiles loose
in their bedrooms

Exile to an island
with no TV

Make them eat
school dinners

Dump them in
snakepits

Drop them in
vats of glop

ZOMBIE VAMPIRE GUIDE

Psssst. You can't be too careful.
Here is my definitive list of how
to tell if anyone you know is a
zombie vampire.

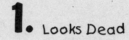

1. Looks Dead

2. Eats Human Flesh

3. Scary Bulging Eyes

4. Big Huge
Tombstone Teeth

5. Loves Bandages

6. Hates Sunlight

7. Drinks Blood

8. Looks like the Walking Dead

9. Says MWWAAAAAAHHHAHHA a lot

10. Also says RAAAAAA and UHHHHHHRRRRGHH

What To Do If Someone You Know Turns into a Zombie Vampire.

RUN!

Henry's Top Ten best EVER tricks

1. Scaring the Best Boys Club into giving me all their money by pretending there was a Fangmangler monster in the garden.

2. Telling Peter that a cardboard box was a time machine and making him think he'd travelled to the future.

3. Grabbing everyone's Halloween sweets despite being stuck at home.

4. Getting rid of Greasy Greta, the Demon Dinner Lady, by putting hot chilli powder in her biscuits.

5. Tricking Bossy Bill into photocopying his bottom.

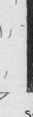 

6. Switching the present tags on Stuck-Up Steve's gifts and mine, so that I got Steve's great gifts and Steve got my horrible ones.

7. Persuading Bossy Bill and Stuck-Up Steve to wear pyjamas for a paintballing party.

8. Escaping from Moody Margaret's school by telling her mum me and Peter had been sick.

9. Terrifying Stuck-Up Steve into thinking there was a monster under his bed.

10. Showing the Bogey Babysitter who's boss by frightening her with a spider in a jar.

Henry's Best Babysitter Rules

1.

Must let children stay up as late as they want

2.

Must let children watch scary movies

3. Children to control the TV remote

4. Unlimited ice cream and sweets

5. All younger brothers and sisters sent to bed IMMEDIATELY

HORRiD HENRY'S
Top Triumphs Fact File

* *

Stealing all the
chocolate
from Peter's
Pirate Party

Making Bossy Bill
leave the school

Escaping from
Milksop Miles
and the
Happy Nappy

Beating Moody
Margaret to
become school
president

Vote Henry
OR ELSE!

Waking the Dead
(well maybe not 100%
awake, but pretty close)

Winning the
Sports Day race

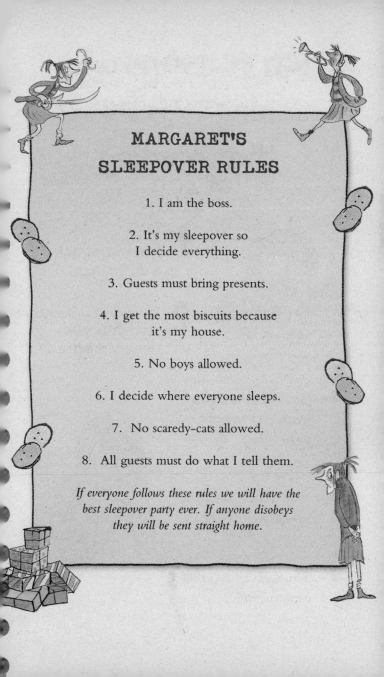

MARGARET'S
SLEEPOVER RULES

1. I am the boss.

2. It's my sleepover so
I decide everything.

3. Guests must bring presents.

4. I get the most biscuits because
it's my house.

5. No boys allowed.

6. I decide where everyone sleeps.

7. No scaredy-cats allowed.

8. All guests must do what I tell them.

*If everyone follows these rules we will have the
best sleepover party ever. If anyone disobeys
they will be sent straight home.*

Ten reasons why watching TV is better than reading

1. Holding a book is very tiring

2. Turning pages is very tiring

3. Moving your eyes from left to right is very tiring

4. You can eat crisps while watching TV

5. You can chat while watching TV

6. You can do your homework while watching TV

7. You can play computer games and watch TV at the same time

8. You can dance while watching TV

9. There are great programmes on TV, like *Hog House* and *Knight Fight* and *Terminator Gladiator*

10. No one ever tests you about what you watched on TV

HORRID HENRY'S
Nature Guide

Every time you step off a concrete
path you are leaving civilisation!
The countryside is full of dangers.

You will meet:

wild beasts

dangerous paths

swollen rivers

stinging nettles

rampaging chickens

quicksand

horrible smells

mud

zombies

vampires

BEWARE!
FRESH AIR.

mummies...

Take it from me — don't leave town.
Remember what happened to Hansel and
Gretel! It could happen to you!
Stay at home and watch TV.

HORRiD HENRY'S Story Writing Tips

1. Nothing boring.

No one wants to read a story called *My Favourite Hot Water Bottle* or *I Love My Radiator*. Remember, scary is always best. Who wouldn't want to know all about KING HENRY THE HORRIBLE or QUEEN GERTRUDE THE GRUESOME or EVIL EVIE AND THE TYRANT TEACHER.

2. Write mash-ups.

Romance? Animals? Princesses? BORING!! But … why not write about an alien who falls in love with a turtle, or a vampire princess who turns into a bumble bee, or a ghost romance, or an animal sports day. Or … no, I'm keeping the best idea for me.

3. Steal good ideas.

It's so much easier to copy someone else. Just do a few quick switches and – bingo! – you've written your story with loads of time left over to watch telly and eat crisps. If I could turn the worst story ever written, Peter's *Butterfly Fairies Paint the Rainbow*, into an exciting adventure about giants stomping about, so can you.

4. In fact, if you make every story all about ME you're guaranteed to write a good one.

Henry's Skeleton Skunk Story

**Skeleton Skunk meets Terminator Gladiator.
May the smelliest fighter win!!!!!!!**

Peeeeuuuwww. What a stink. What a smell. What
a pong. The smelliest skunkiest fighter burst into
the shop. He looked around at the terrified faces.

'All right, where is he?' snarled Skeleton Skunk.
'Where's that so-called Gladiator who calls
himself Terminator? Because he is about to
be terminated. Ahaha ha ha ha.'

'He ain't here, Skunk,' quivered the man
behind the counter. 'Honest.'

'A likely story,' jeered Skeleton Skunk.

'No one's seen him,' said the man, shivering.

'That's 'cause he's a yellow-livered coward,'
sneered Skeleton Skunk, 'and when I find
him—'

'Who are you calling coward?' hissed a
voice from the ceiling.

Skeleton Skunk looked up. There, swinging from the chandelier, was Terminator Gladiator.

Ooops, thought the Skunk. His bones rattled. Oooops. Time for my top secret super-skunky plan . . .

by Henry

HORRID HENRY'S Bedtime Thoughts

No one ever wants to go to bed (unless you're a baby nappy-face wormy toad like Peter). But sometimes you've got no choice . . . so here's some great things to think about to help you fall asleep.

1. Count zombies

2. Count marauding goats

3. Think about the monster hiding under your bed

4. Think about the monsters hiding in your wardrobe

5. Listen to all the scary creaks on the stairs

6. Remember the scary vampire story you saw on TV

7. Wonder if your bathroom is haunted

8. Imagine werewolves trying to smash their way into your room

9. Remember that really spooky ghost story

10. Imagine being chased by a gigantic spider

Trust me, you'll be asleep before you know it.

HORRiD HENRY'S
Super-Secret
Purple Hand Fort
Passwords

Wibble Pants

Nappy baby

Bibble

Frog-Face

Noodle Head

Mr Kill

Nunga

Terminator

TOP SECRET
PHRASE BOOK

Peter is smelly = **Hi!**

Peter is a worm = **Give me all your pocket money.**

Nappy-Face Toad = **I want biscuits.**

Peter is the Duke of Poop = **Goodbye!**

Example:

Peter is smelly. Peter is a worm.
Peter is the Duke of Poop.

means

Hi! Give me all your pocket money. Goodbye!

(So I'm NOT calling Peter names. I'm just talking in code.)

SECRET CLUB

Rules

No boys allowed
Margaret: Leader
Susan: Spy
Gurinder: biscuits and trainee spy
Linda: biscuits

Password: Nunga
Motto: Down with boys

PURPLE HAND FORT

RULES

No girls allowed
Henry: Leader
Ralph: Deputy Leader.
Peter: Sentry (junior)
Henry's Title: Lord High Excellent Majesty
Peters Title: Worm

Peters must bow to Henry and Ralph
Peter must never touch the Purple hand Skull and
crossbones biscuit tin
Peter not allowed in the Purple Hand Fort
without Henry's permission
Peter is a tempory member only.
Password: Smelly Toads
Motto: Down with girls

Check out another story
you might like…

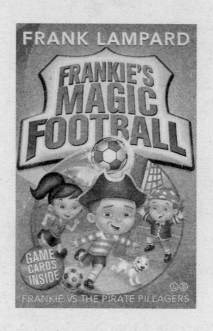

"Have we got time for a kickabout?" asked Louise, nodding to the park gates opposite the funfair.

Frankie checked his watch. Ten past five. *There's always time for football,* he thought. "Maybe for ten minutes."

They ran into the park. At first,

Frankie thought it was completely empty. Then a voice called out: "Look who it is, Kev!"

Frankie turned around and saw his brother Kevin with two of his friends. They were leaning against a fence, drinking cans of energy drink.

"Cool ball, Frank*enstein*," said Kevin. He laughed at his lame joke, downed his drink, then dropped the can on the grass.

"Let's leave them to it," muttered Charlie.

But Frankie's blood was boiling. "You should put that in the bin, Kev," he said.

"Oh?" said his brother. "You gonna tell Mum?"

Frankie stared at him. He knew full well that if their mum *could* see what Kevin had done, she'd drag him home by his ear.

Frankie walked towards his brother, then stooped to get the can. If Kevin wouldn't put it in the bin, he would. But at the last moment, his brother kicked the can out of reach. "Nice try," he sniggered. Frankie reached again, and Kev dribbled it away, laughing. "Too slow, Frankenstein!" he said.

"That's enough," said Louise.

Kevin lifted his foot to kick the

can away. "Hey!" he shouted, as Max charged in. The little dog snapped up the can in his jaws and ran off. Kevin lost his balance as he swung his leg and fell on his backside. Max trotted to a bin, stood on his hind paws and dropped the can in.

Frankie managed to keep a straight face, but Kevin's friends burst out laughing.

"Great skills!" said one of them.

"Tackled by a dog, man!" said the other.

Kevin clambered to his feet, blushing bright red. His jeans had a dark grass stain on the back and he turned angrily to Frank. "You'd better not be late for tea!" he said, and stormed off. His friends followed.

"Or what?" Frankie called after him jokingly. "You gonna tell Mum?" He gave Max another treat. "We'd better make this a quick game," he said to the others.

"There!" said Charlie, pointing to a climbing frame shaped like a model ship. He jogged over and stood in front of it. "The ship's the goal."

Frankie booted the ball high into the air. Max streaked after it. It tangled in his feet, and he tumbled over the top.

"Pass it!" called Frankie.

Max managed to nose the ball to Louise. She dribbled the ball in and out of the swings, then sent a curling shot towards the top corner of the goal. Charlie dived and just got his fingertips to the ball.

"Nothing gets past me!" said Charlie.

We'll see about that . . . thought Frankie. He fetched the ball and passed it to Louise. She looked up, ready to shoot, then stepped over the ball and flicked it up with her heel. Frankie was ready. He brought his foot round and connected with a perfect volley. The ball screamed towards the goal. Charlie leapt sideways, gloves splayed, but the ball passed beneath his outstretched hands. Frankie slid on to his knees, thinking his mum would kill him when she saw the grass stains.

"SUPERGOA . . ."

The shout trailed off in Frankie's throat.

The ball had vanished, and so had the model ship. Max growled quietly. Frankie stood up, his heart thumping. He couldn't believe what was before his eyes.

Where the goal had been just a second before was a swirl of light like nothing he'd ever seen. Colours flashed and spun in a disc shape, three metres across. He looked at Louise. Her jaw had dropped open.

Charlie picked himself up, bashing the ground with his fist. He still hadn't seen the spinning circle of light behind him. "I was so close!" he said.

"Er, Charlie," said Louise. "You might want to turn around."

He did as she told him, then leapt backwards. "Holy moly! What is that thing?"

BOOK IN
FOR YOUR NEW ADVENTURE TODAY

CELEBRATING
WORLD
BOOK
DAY
2 MARCH 2017

3 brilliant ways to continue YOUR reading adventure

1 VISIT YOUR LOCAL BOOKSHOP

Your go-to destination for awesome reading recommendations and events with your favourite authors and illustrators.

 Booksellers.org.uk/bookshopsearch

2 JOIN YOUR LOCAL LIBRARY

Browse and borrow from a huge selection of books, get expert ideas of what to read next, and take part in wonderful family reading activities – all for FREE!

 Findalibrary.co.uk

3 DISCOVER A WORLD OF STORIES ONLINE

32 podcasts to try

Stuck for ideas of what to read next? Plug yourself in to our brilliant new podcast library! Sample a world of amazing books, brought to life by amazing storytellers. **worldbookday.com**

HAPPY BIRTHDAY WORLD BOOK DAY!

Let's celebrate...

Can you believe this year is our **20th birthday** – and thanks to you, as well as our amazing authors, illustrators, booksellers, librarians and teachers, there's SO much to celebrate!

Did you know that since WORLD BOOK DAY began in 1997, we've given away over **275 million book tokens**? WOW! We're delighted to have brought so many books directly into the hands of millions of children and young people just like you, with a gigantic assortment of fun activities and events and resources and quizzes and dressing-up and games too – we've even broken a **Guinness World Record**!

Whether you love discovering books that make you **laugh**, CRY, *hide under the covers* or **drive your imagination wild**, with WORLD BOOK DAY, there's always something for everyone to choose–as well as ideas for exciting new books to try at bookshops, libraries and schools everywhere.

And as a small charity, we couldn't do it without a lot of help from our friends in the publishing industry and our brilliant sponsor, NATIONAL BOOK TOKENS. Hip-hip hooray to them and three cheers to you, our readers and everyone else who has joined us over the last 20 years to make WORLD BOOK DAY happen.

Happy Birthday to us – and happy reading to you!

#WorldBookDay20